First published in 2018
by Jessica Kingsley Publishers
73 Collier Street
London N1 9BE, UK
and
400 Market Street, Suite 400
Philadelphia, PA 19106, USA

www.jkp.com

Front cover image source: Richy K. Chandler

Fonts used: Richy Wide and Richy Magik, both designed by the author

Library of Congress Cataloging in Publication Data
A CIP catalog record for this book is available from the Library of Congress

British Library Cataloguing in Publication Data
A CIP catalogue record for this book is available from the British Library

ISBN 978 1 78592 414 9
eISBN 978 1 78450 776 3

Printed and bound in China

For Emir

You Make Your Parents
SUPER HAPPY!

A book about parents separating

Written and illustrated by
RICHY K. CHANDLER

Jessica Kingsley Publishers
London and Philadelphia

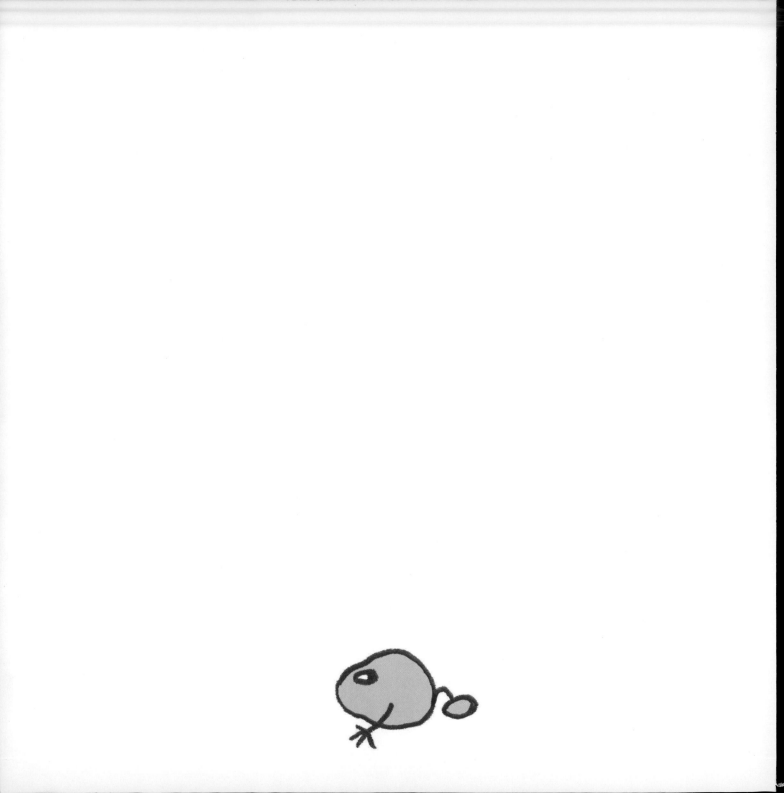

Hey!

I think you should know,

there is nothing
your parents are
more proud of...

...than YOU!

You make them
SUPER HAPPY!

More than
ice-cream,

or
puppies,

or
sunny
days.

BUT...

Your parents don't agree on everything.

Sometimes they make each other really upset,

...and really ANGRY.

While they've tried
hard to get along,

...they realised that if they stayed living in the same place, things would get very unhappy for everyone.

So they decided it was better to live in two separate homes,

...and that seems
a bit scary...

pretty sad...

...and certainly not what you were expecting...

So they make sure that they both see you lots,

and
read you
stories,

and take you to fun places!

So even though your parents don't agree on everything, the one thing they are both sure of is that you are AMAZING...

and they both love you

with all their hearts!

And whatever they do...

...and whatever you do...

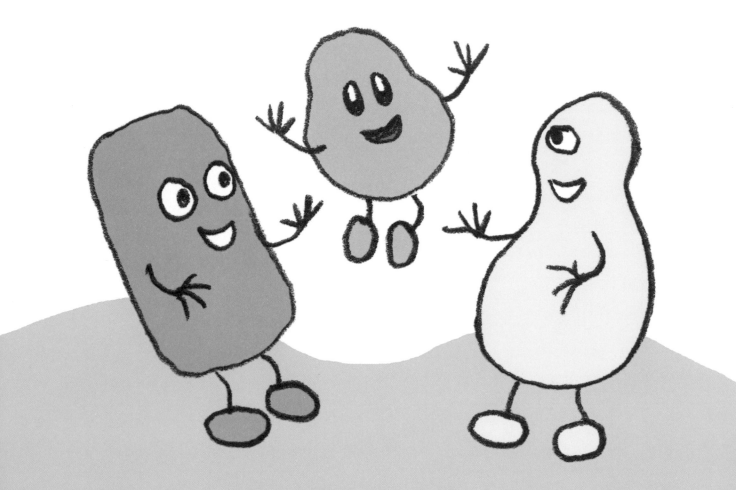

...that will never change.

Richy K. Chandler
is a writer, illustrator and comic maker.

He is the creator of webcomic *Lucy the Octopus* and *WASP (Webcomic Artist Swap Project)*, and co-creator of fairytale manga *Rosie and Jacinda*. His comic publishing imprint, Tempo Lush, has released two *Tempo Lush Tales* anthologies, which Richy conceived and edited as well as contributing writing and artwork. Richy is also the author and illustrator of the graphic novel *When Are You Going to Get a Proper Job?* published by Jessica Kingsley Publishers.

Richy has worked as a freelancer for Titan Comics, both writing (*Almost Naked Animals, Wallace & Gromit, Adventure Time*) and drawing (Dreamworks' *Home*). He also illustrated Apples and Snakes' *The No Panic Book of Not Panicking*.

Richy runs comic workshops for children and adults, and shares a studio with a cat who always tries to steal his snacks.

tempolush.com
lucytheoctopus.net

These organisations can offer support and
advice to families going through separation...

Family Lives
www.familylives.org.uk

Family Rights Group
www.frg.org.uk

Only Dads
www.onlydads.org

Only Mums
www.onlymums.org

Sorting Out Separation
www.sortingoutseparation.org.uk

The Parent Connection
www.theparentconnection.org.uk